WITHAM
09/25

WITHDRAWN

WITHDRAWN

Please return this book on or before the date shown above. To renew go to www.essex.gov.uk/libraries, ring 0345 603 7628 or go to any Essex library.

Essex County Council

GW01527299

Essex County Council

3013030705381 8

Lonely Planet Kids

Good Night, Earth

5-MINUTE STORIES ABOUT NATURE AFTER DARK

Rose Davidson &
Ester Gouw

Contents

Introduction	6

THE SUN SETS — 8
The Wandering Hippo — 10
Dance of the Starlings — 16
Koala Comfort — 22
Snow Much Fun — 28

GETTING COSY — 34
The Orangutan's New Nest — 36
Safe and Sound — 42
Dreaming in the Den — 48
Home at Last — 54

WIDE AWAKE — 60
Eyes on the Prize — 62
The Chase Is On — 68
Life in the Shadows — 74
A Fancy Feast — 80
A Wild Ride — 86

LIGHTS ON! — 92
Firefly Flashes — 94
The Bay That Glows — 100
Ghost Mushrooms — 106
Mighty Mounds — 112

TIME TO GROW   118
- The Rimu's Rare Berries   120
- Blooms for Bats   126
- A Sparkling Surprise   132
- Short and Sweet   138

A MIDNIGHT SKY   144
- Into the Sea   146
- Roll With It   152
- Painted Skies   158
- A Magical Mist   164

Say "Good Night"
Around the World   170
Did You Know...?   172
Glossary   174
Index   175
Credits   176

Introduction

As daylight fades to darkened skies, and sleepy heads hit their pillows, the world is waking up in a whole new way. Rainforests hum to life with hungry creatures big and small. Animals dart across the sandy desert and creep through the shadowy trees. The moon's gentle light guides critters on their paths, while a curious bay offers a glowing gift.

If you've ever wondered what happens while you're asleep, snuggle up and get ready to uncover some of nature's best-kept secrets. As you explore, you'll meet orangutans preparing for bedtime in the trees, follow busy bats on a midnight quest, and discover magical nighttime blooms. You'll also witness some quieter moments of beauty, including fireflies twinkling through the air and the sky performing a peaceful, dazzling dance of colours.

The 25 stories in this book come from all over the globe. As night unfolds, each chapter reveals new surprises. You can start your journey from the beginning with sunset stories or choose where you want to go first! Take a look at the map to see where each story takes place.

Alaska, United States
P. 48

Canada
P. 28

North America

New York City, United States
P. 80

Texas, United States
P. 138

Costa Rica
P. 62

Ecuador
P. 126

South America

Ema
Natio
Par
Braz
P. 1

The Sun Sets

When the glowing sun sinks lower in the sky, the sky starts to change colours. Around the world, the disappearing light signals animals to prepare for sleep, eat or play.

Good Night, Earth

The Wandering Hippo

Okavango Delta, Botswana
Africa

The sun goes down on the African savanna, painting the sky vibrant shades of yellow, orange and red. The air gets slightly cooler with the fading sun.

A herd of hippos is resting in the river. For them, staying in the water is the only way to keep cool on hot days. Outside the water, their skin will get dry and cracked under the heat of the sun. They might even get a sunburn.

In the rainy season, there is much more water here. Floods fill the river and make it wider. It is now the dry season, and the river is narrower. Along the banks of the river, lush grass grows. The hippos snack on the grass.

The Wandering Hippo

As night falls and the temperature cools, the hungry hippos begin to emerge from the water. One by one, they lumber onto land. The largest male comes out first. He's the leader of the herd. Other adults follow him to shore. The youngest hippo waits until last for its turn to exit.

Slowly, the adults begin their nightly walk to graze for more grass. *Thud. Thud. Thud. Thud.* Each stomp of the hippos' large feet makes a thundering sound. They have travelled this path many times before. They follow the path they've worn in the ground.

This is the young hippo's first time grazing with the herd. The hippo was born in the water just a few months ago. Until now, he's fed off his mother's milk, bobbing underwater to drink it.

But before the young hippo can exit the water, something unexpected happens. A crocodile, who's been lurking in the water nearby, has set its sights on the hippo. Seeing that the hippo is alone in the water, the crocodile takes its chance to strike. It lunges towards the young hippo, its jaws wide open and ready to chomp.

The mother hippo sees the crocodile move towards her baby. Quickly, she doubles back into the water. Her mouth is wide open, showing her massive teeth. The threat of a hippo bite is scary enough to make the crocodile give up. But the young hippo is also scared. He dashes out of the water and onto land, not looking back. Finally, when he can't run anymore, the young hippo looks up. The rest of his herd is nowhere in sight.

Now safe from danger, the brave young hippo starts to calm down. He looks around, taking in his new surroundings. Tall grasses sprawl as far as the eye can see. Giant acacia trees dot the seemingly never-ending landscape. In the distance, a group of giraffes munch on the trees' leaves. The hippo bends down to eat some grass. *Ah, finally,* he thinks.

The sky is getting lighter. *Time is running out*, thinks the young hippo. He must return to the water before the sun rises. When morning comes, the sun will be too hot. But how?

Suddenly, the young hippo hears a noise. "Honk!" The voice is familiar. *It's Mum!* thinks the young hippo. "Honk!" He lets out a loud noise in return. His mother starts to race towards him. Soon, the two are reunited.

The mother hippo leads her baby back to the path. Together, they follow the track back to the river. As they walk, the moon lights their way. Finally, they dip back into the river to join the rest of the herd.

Dance of the Starlings

**ROME, ITALY
EUROPE**

The setting sun casts a warm glow across a farmer's olive grove. Just outside the hustle and bustle of Rome, hundreds of neat rows of olive trees dot the land. Amid the trees, a starling is finding a tasty snack.

It's winter, and the starling has travelled a long way to get to the farm. So have many other starlings. Hundreds of starlings, also taking refuge after their long migration, are scattered across the farm. As the sky changes from orange to a cotton-candy pink, the black-and-white speckled birds are ready to explore their warmer winter home.

Just then, a falcon flies overhead. It spooks the starlings. Row by row, they take off to avoid the predator. *There is power in numbers,* thinks the starling. Together, they can confuse the bigger bird.

The starlings fly away from the farm, making their way towards the centre of the city. Along the way, more and more starlings join the flight. They stick close together, forming a massive dark cloud in the pink sky.

As they fly, the starlings watch one another, picking up on every tiny move. The starling from the olive farm, all alone before, now watches the movements of the birds beside it. Without missing a beat, it copies each movement.

Now, the flock of starlings moves in perfect harmony.

Swoop!

The birds swiftly drop down towards the arena. They beat their wings as they arc to the side. Then they whizz high into the sky. Together, they look like a waterfall of wings cascading through the air.

Swish!

As the starlings approach the stony ruins of Rome, they gather above the Colosseum, an ancient site where Roman gladiators famously once duelled. By now, the sun has almost sunk below the horizon. The birds stop their dance and look for somewhere to rest. They find a place to perch in the nearby trees.

While the starlings rest, locals finish their dinners and emerge to take an evening stroll. People fill the piazzas as they chat with each other about their days. During this time of year, some people carry umbrellas with them. But not because rain might fall . . . because something else might!

Here in the city, the starlings are famed for more than their dancing. They're also known for their many pounds of poop that covers the sidewalks as they rest in the trees overhead. Although the starlings' droppings are an unwelcome sight and smell, their dance in the sky is a stunning spectacle to see.

Koala Comfort

New South Wales
Australia

Amid a forest of eucalyptus trees, a koala is settling into her new home. She rests in the crook of a tree, just a few feet from the ground. It was the first tree she saw when she arrived, and she leapt into it quickly, hopping like a frog up the tree's trunk. For hours, she has been snacking on its eucalyptus leaves, plucking them from nearby branches with her strong hands. But now, the tree is almost bare.

The koala travelled far to live in this forest. Recently, a wildfire destroyed the forest where she once lived. She had to act fast to flee from the trees and avoid the blaze. She managed to escape just in time.

Once the blaze had died down, caring humans rescued her from the charred forest. They loaded her into a large wooden box and secured the box onto a truck. Then, they drove her to this forest, where fires have never touched the trees. They hauled the box off of the truck and set it down near the tasty eucalyptus trees. When they opened the door, the koala leapt out and entered her new home.

Now, the sun over her new home has almost disappeared. She twists and turns her body, hoping to settle into a comfy spot. As the restless koala wriggles around, her stomach starts to grumble. She looks around, but there are no more leaves within reach. *Uh-oh!* the koala thinks. And she's still not comfortable.

The hungry koala wraps her arms around the sturdy trunk of the eucalyptus tree. Bottom first, she lowers herself towards the ground. *Plop!* Her body reaches the forest floor.

Koala Comfort

The koala turns her belly towards the ground and stands on all fours. She begins to walk away. With a body made for life in the trees, her legs move slowly and awkwardly on land. As one front leg moves, the opposite back leg moves.

Soon, she comes to the base of another tree. She looks up. *Nope, this one is taken!* she thinks as she sees another koala in the tree. She continues walking. The next tree is taken, too, and so is the one after that.

Finally, the koala spots an empty tree, lush with lots of leaves. *Perfect!* she thinks. *This is the one.* She gets ready to climb.

The koala extends the long, sharp claws inside her paws and sinks them into the bark to get a firm grip on the tree. She moves her left paw higher, sinking her claws back into the bark. Then, she moves the right paws higher. With each move, she uses her strong legs to push herself up the trunk.

At last, she crawls into the crook of the new tree. Now, she can rest. She is so tired, she has forgotten she wanted a snack! The koala quickly drifts to sleep.

Snow Much Fun

CANADA
NORTH AMERICA

A golden sky burns over a snow-covered hill in Canada. At the base of the hill, where the land meets the river, a family of river otters is gathering their dinner. The mother otter comes up from the water with her daily catch. It's a large catfish! *Chomp, chomp, chomp.* They all bite into the fish. She holds down the fish with her front paws while her three pups finish taking bites. They eat until their bellies are full.

After dinner, the pups are ready to play. They turn to look up at the hill, then back to each other. *Race you to the top!* thinks one pup and starts to run. Just like that, the race is on.

The young otters scurry as fast as they can through the fresh, powdery snow. Their paws sink into the snow as they run. Soon enough, they all reach the top of the hill. Here, the playful otters see the river below. They also see their mum waiting patiently for them to return. She looks much smaller from way up here!

The otters form a line on the hilltop. The oldest goes first. He runs a few steps, then plops down to the ground. He pushes his belly into the snow and pulls his paws up towards the sky. Then he leans forwards and glides down the hill. *Whee!* He picks up speed, moving closer and closer to the river. As he travels along, his body carves a natural slide into the snow.

As her brother reaches the middle of the hill, the second otter prepares to slide. She makes her own running start, then glides down on her belly.

Next, it's the youngest otter's turn. He, too, begins to glide on his belly. But, being the smallest, he doesn't pick up as much speed. He starts to slow down, then comes to a stop. *Not a problem!* thinks the little otter. He quickly stands up, runs a few more steps, and plops back onto his belly. *Whee!*

Finally, all of the otters reach the base of the hill. Back along the riverbank, the otters jump into the water. They twist and dive. One otter chases another otter's tail.

As night falls, the otters crawl out of the river to dry off. Then their mum leads them to a hollow tree nearby. One by one, the pups crawl into the tree. They snuggle together and drift off to sleep.

Getting Cosy

A darkened sky signals bedtime for some creatures. Animal families snuggle into their nests, burrows and dens, preparing for a good night's sleep.

Good Night, Earth

The Orangutan's New Nest

Borneo, Indonesia
Southeast Asia

It's a sunny afternoon in the Bornean rainforest. A soft breeze tickles the tropical tree leaves. In the bushy canopy, a mother orangutan climbs through the densely packed branches high above the forest floor. With strong little hands, her 10-month-old baby boy clings to the coarse red hair on her belly. On his head, a frizzled mess of hair sticks straight into the sky.

Around them, the forest is abuzz with other creatures. A pair of rhinoceros hornbills beat their wings as they flit from branch to branch. A Siamese crocodile lurks in the murky waters of a river. By the water's edge, a group of proboscis monkeys gather in a tree to groom each other.

The Orangutan's New Nest

The young ape's eyes are wide with wonder. He watches his surroundings as his mother guides him through the trees. He needs to learn his way around because, one day, he will travel these trees alone. But today, he takes in the forest from the safety of his mother's arms.

Since dawn, the two orangutans have been travelling in search of food. The mother ape shows her baby what to eat and how to catch it. *Shwoop!* He watches as his mother quickly plucks a juicy insect from a branch. Today, they've also found a special treat: Mum picks a spiky durian fruit from a tree. After pulling some leaves from a nearby tree, she covers the fruit to protect her hands. Then, she rips it open. She eats the fleshy fruit and – *ptooey!* – spits out the seeds.

Good Night, Earth

Now, the sun is setting and it's time to rest. But the orangutans are far from last night's nest.

Mum scans the forest for a safe, cosy place to sleep. Soon, she sets her eyes on a large, sturdy branch. Carefully, with her baby back on her belly, she climbs to it. Facing the tree's massive trunk, she follows the branch down to the crook. *This looks like the perfect spot,* she thinks. She plops down on the branch and leans against the trunk. From here, she can see for miles. She places her baby safely beside her. Then, she gets to work on building a new nest.

Mum doesn't have to go far to get the supplies she needs. She reaches for the long, flexible branches just beside her and bends them towards her body. Raindrops roll off the branches' leaves and onto the forest floor below. The recent rain has made the branches soft and easier to bend. Using her nimble fingers, she carefully weaves the branches together to form a large bowl.

The Orangutan's New Nest

Now, she grabs some smaller twigs and arranges them evenly around the bowl. Finally, it's time to add the leaves. Soon, a soft padding fills the nest. *Ta-da!* After a few minutes, the pair have a comfy bed for the night. Mum rolls into the nest to test it out.

The baby has been watching his mum at work. Taking note, he grabs a small leafy twig. He waves the twig above his head. *This is fun!* thinks the baby ape. Then, oops! The ape slips and slides on the wet branch. Suddenly, he's under the branch, hanging by one hand. The forest floor is far away. The ape needs a helping hand, and fast!

Mum doesn't hesitate. She swings her hand down and grabs hold of the young ape's arm. Slowly, she lifts him back up and pulls him towards the fresh, cosy nest. Still holding him by the arm, she lowers him down until his body meets the leafy mattress.

Unshaken, the young ape is happy to test out the new nest, just like Mum did. He stretches and rolls back and forth, trying to find the comfiest way to lie. Sensing her son's restlessness, the mother wraps her arms around her baby and the young ape settles in. Growing tired, he fights to keep his eyes open. Mum reaches for another leafy branch and folds it in, laying it on top like a blanket. Soon, the two are slowly drifting to sleep.

The rainforest has grown quiet and dark. The only sounds are the chirping of insects and the peaceful flow of the river's running water. Tomorrow, the two will travel again, search for more food, and leave this bed behind. They'll make a new nest somewhere else. But there is nothing left to see or do today. For now, all that's left to do is sleep.

Safe and Sound

Kalahari Desert
Southern Africa

In the dry heat of the Kalahari Desert, dozens of meerkats are relaxing together outside their burrow. Many of the adult meerkats, seeing the blazing sun sink closer towards the dusty red earth, are returning from their daily hunt. Back at the burrow, they rejoin their group, called a mob. Some of the adults have stayed at the burrow all day, babysitting the youngest meerkats.

One meerkat has come back from her hunt with a special treat: a scorpion! She's removed the stinger so her pup can munch on it without getting stung. She carries the scorpion's body in her mouth, then drops it in front of her pup. Dinner is served!

Safe and Sound

Around the burrow, the meerkats start getting ready for bed. One meerkat grooms another, using its claws and teeth to brush the bugs from its fur. Others lean back to soak in the last rays of the day's sun. Some of the younger meerkats tumble and play around in the dirt, getting out some extra energy before they settle in to sleep.

At nighttime, most of the meerkats go to their rooms. But one meerkat has a special job. He watches for predators, such as birds or snakes, that might try to enter the burrow. The meerkat guards the burrow from the outside so he can keep an eye out for these predators. If he sees or hears one, he must let the others know – quickly and loudly!

Good Night, Earth

Now it's time for a new guard to start his watch and give the other guard a rest. The new guard climbs to the top of a high rock near the burrow. He stands on his hind legs to get a good view. Then he sends out a loud peeping sound that tells the others, "I'm on duty!" Every few seconds, he lets out another sound. Each time, the sound tells the others that there is no danger and they are safe.

Safe and Sound

The other meerkats cuddle up in their underground burrow as they get ready to sleep. Under the ground, the meerkats stay cool from the heat. Some 40 meerkats can fit inside! Most of them are brothers and sisters. The adults take turns caring for the pups. Together, the mob will teach the pups to hunt for food, clean, and defend their burrow.

The burrow has many entrances and rooms connected by tunnels. There is even a special bathroom. There are also lots of bedrooms where the meerkats sleep, snuggling together.

Good Night, Earth

Almost an hour has passed, and most of the meerkats are fast asleep. Back aboveground, the guard detects movement in a tree. A cobra is slithering down the trunk, and it's coming straight for the burrow!

"Bark!" "Bark, bark!" He alerts the others. The rest of the meerkats wake up and jump into action. They run out of a special hole designed for a quick getaway.

SAFE AND SOUND

The meerkats emerge from the burrow and charge at the snake. Working as a team, they form a circle around the intruder. The cobra raises its head. The meerkats in front of the snake stand tall as they face off with the threat. Behind the snake, other meerkats start nipping at its back. Ouch! The snake gives up and slithers away.

Phew! thinks the guard. A new guard takes over for the next hour-long shift. The rest of the meerkats return to their burrow and settle in again for bed.

Dreaming in the Den

ALASKA, UNITED STATES
NORTH AMERICA

At the Katmai National Park and Preserve in Alaska, a flurry of snowflakes falls from the sky. The flakes tumble down and come to rest on the blanket of soft, fluffy snow that already covers the ground.

Inside the slope of a mountain, a brown bear has made her den. Here, in the middle of winter, she gave birth to two cubs. Weighing less than a pound each, the babies were hairless and blind. They rely on mum to feed them and keep them safe.

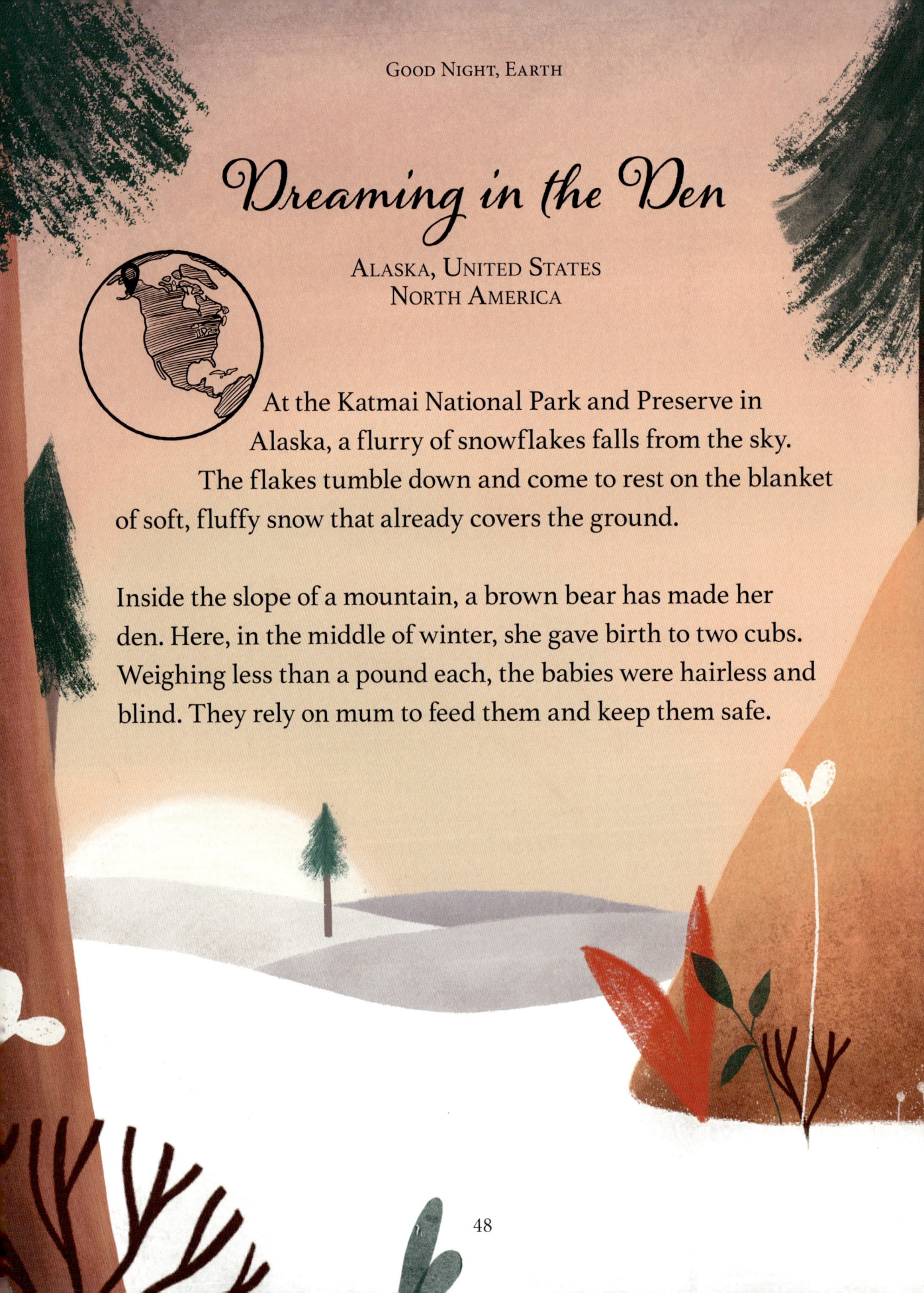

The mum and her cubs are curled up for warmth. The cubs, now three months old, have never seen the world beyond the den. They must grow bigger and stronger before they are ready to leave. Out there, the tiny cubs are vulnerable to bigger mammals, such as wolves.

The mother bear hasn't eaten since she arrived in the den. Her body has been feeding on the fat she stored up from her summer feast. In the den, she spends most of the day sleeping to save energy. She only wakes up to tend to her cubs. As she rests, she remembers one of her last big meals.

It was a hot day in late summer when she trekked to the Brooks River. Just like many other brown bears, she comes to this river each summer. She knows that it will be filled with fish!

Dreaming in the Den

The fish are sockeye salmon. Each summer, they swim from the ocean up the river to lay their eggs. At one part of the river, there is a waterfall. This is Brooks Falls. Here, the salmon must leap up and over the fall to reach the other side of the river.

That summer day, the mama bear stood on the short ledge of the waterfall, peering down at the water below. Suddenly, a salmon leapt out of the water and into the air! She opened her mouth wide to catch it. But the fish was just out of reach. The fish dunked back into the water and swam away.

Then, another salmon leapt into the air. *Chomp. Squish!* This time, she caught it! She sunk her teeth into the fish's head, then carried it upstream. With both paws, she gripped the fish's body while she chomped. Then, she went back to the falls for another bite. In just one day, she caught dozens of fish.

Dreaming in the Den

A cry from one of her cubs wakes the mother bear from her slumber. She pulls her cubs close to feed them. *In a few months,* she thinks, *I will teach my cubs to fish.*

Good Night, Earth

Home at Last

Falkland Islands
South America

On a small island just above Antarctica, a young Magellanic penguin emerges from the water. *Pop!* The penguin pokes his head above the water's surface. Slowly, dripping wet, he waddles onto the sandy shore, where more penguins are gathered. It's a penguin reunion!

Home at Last

The tired penguin has been swimming for more than 6,000 kilometres. Along with many other penguins, he just swam all the way from the northern part of South America, where he spent the winter to escape the bitter cold in Antarctica. But this isn't the first time he has been to this island. Just like his parents, he was born on this beach!

A few days pass as more penguins show up at the beach and mingle together. All around, returning penguins greet their friends. "Bray!" A penguin lets out a loud donkey-like sound. She is calling out to her friend. Although it's been many months, the friend recognises the penguin's voice. She waddles through the crowd to reach her.

A young penguin looks around. This is his first time returning to the island since birth. Others have been here many times before. He doesn't have friends yet, or a nest of his own. He is lonely, so he introduces himself. He lets out his own loud sound. "Brayyy!"

Nearby, another young penguin hears his call. She waddles towards the sound. The penguin walks around her a few times to say hello. Then, he pats her with his flippers. *Now we're friends!* he thinks.

Good Night, Earth

Together, they waddle away from the beach, towards a grassy hillside. Looking up, they see hundreds of holes dotting the slopes. Each one is a nest. They look for an open space on the hill to build their nest. Once they find a good spot, they lie on their bellies and dig into the soil with their feet.

Home at Last

Once their nest is made, the two young penguins crawl inside. The friends groom each other before closing their eyes. Someday soon, they may be sitting on an egg, keeping it warm until it hatches. Tonight, with their long journey finally complete, they rest.

Wide Awake

While some animals are going to sleep, the setting sun spurs other animals to action. These animals are nocturnal – they are awake at night. They explore, hunt, eat and bond under the cover of darkness.

Eyes on the Prize

**COSTA RICA
CENTRAL AMERICA**

A mist fills the air as a strong, heavy rain pours from the pitch-black sky. *Pitter-patter. Pitter-patter.* Droplets of water bounce from the leaves of the rainforest canopy. They roll down and soak the forest floor below.

A few months ago, a red-eyed tree frog laid dozens of eggs on one of the rainforest leaves. She carefully chose a leaf that was hanging over a pond. The eggs looked like little beads of water glimmering under the setting sun. When the eggs were ready to hatch into tadpoles, the babies wriggled and squirmed free. One by one they rolled off the leaf and – *plunk!* – tumbled directly down into the water.

The tadpoles swam together in the pond, munching on insects in the water. They grew legs and morphed into tiny froglets. Their skin changed from brown to bright green. Their eyes changed from brown to bright red.

The mother frog's job is done and so, with a mighty leap, she jumps clear of the pond. Tonight, one of her tiny frogs will follow her and also leave the pond. "It's time to explore!" thinks the little frog. Until this moment, he's spent all his time with his siblings. Now, he is ready to make his own way in the world.

Slowly moving one back leg towards his head, the frog takes his first step on land. He moves the other back leg, then repeats. Carefully, the frog creeps into the darkened forest. His skin blends in with the plants on the forest floor.

The frog comes to a tangled mess of knobby tree roots. *How will I get across?* he wonders. The roots are tall, and he can't see what lies beyond them. But the frog is brave. He firmly plants one of his front feet on a root. Thinking he needs all his strength, the frog pulls up his body. But he lifts his body up with ease. The frog has sticky toe pads that help him climb!

From the top of the root, the frog sees a line of little green things moving along the ground below. *What are those?* he thinks. *They don't look like frogs!*

It's an army of leafcutter ants. They are hard at work on the forest floor. They've chewed off tiny bits of leaves from the nearby plants. Now, they're carrying the leaves above their heads! The superstrong ants are headed underground. There, they'll use the leaves to make food.

With his sticky toes, the frog climbs up the tree trunk above the roots. As he starts to get the hang of the motions, he moves more quickly. He speeds up the trunk. Then, he senses a presence above him.

A margay is climbing headfirst down the tree. But it's not using sticky toe pads. This animal has claws! The margay sinks her claws into the bark to grip the tree.

The frog moves sideways to get out of the margay's way. He keeps climbing up.

Finally, the frog finds a cosy leaf. He climbs underneath it and sticks his toes to the underside. *I can sleep here,* thinks the frog. He tucks in his orange feet and closes his red eyes. A clear eyelid with golden veins covers the frog's eyes, so the frog can still detect danger while resting.

The tiny frog has had a busy night. In just a few hours, he's learnt so many things about his new home outside the pond. The rainforest isn't just for frogs. So many different animals live here, and each one has its own special skill.

The Chase Is On

Gobi Desert, Mongolia and China
Asia

The blazing heat radiates through the night air in the Gobi Desert. It hasn't rained here in months. The ground is dry and hot to the touch.

Underground, temperatures are cooler. Some animals here make burrows in the ground to stay cool. The long-eared jerboa is one of them.

The jerboa emerges from her burrow in the dusty earth. The furry little rodent looks like something out of a cartoon. She has ears like a rabbit's and back legs like a kangaroo's. Hairs on the rodent's feet keep her tiny paws from slipping on the sand.

The Chase Is On

It's time for the jerboa to eat. She tucks in her short front legs and stands tall on her long back legs. *Boing! Boing, boing!* She sets off into the desert. With each hop, her long, strong tail touches the ground. Her tail helps her balance as she bounces.

Along the edge of the desert, a little owl sits silently, perched on a rock. The owl has incredible eyesight, and from up here, she can see for miles. The owl scans the desert below. She zeroes in on the hopping jerboa.

The owl eats plenty of insects and worms. A jerboa would be a special treat – but the owl must work hard to catch it.

The Chase Is On

The owl studies the jerboa, watching how quickly it moves. Then, *whoosh!* The owl swoops down from its perch. She flaps her wings as quickly as she can. She opens her talons to scoop up her meal. Within seconds, the owl is almost on top of the rodent.

The jerboa's big ears have heard the owl coming. As the owl approaches the ground, the rodent picks up speed and takes a sharp turn to evade the bird. Her feet plunge into the sand, sending dust flying into the air. Zigging and zagging across the sand, the jerboa leaves a trail of dust in her wake.

The owl touches down on the ground behind the jerboa. Her talons scrape the sand, but miss the little animal. The owl flaps its wings again, lifting up into the air empty-handed.

It's time to move on, she thinks. The little owl flies back to the edge of the desert.

The Chase Is On

Meanwhile, the jerboa keeps hopping until she's sure that the owl is gone. Finally, the jerboa rests. Then, she sees an insect flying overhead. With another large leap, the jerboa lunges into the air and catches a snack.

Back at her perch, the little owl scans the desert again. Now it is quiet, with not an animal in sight. *Tonight just wasn't my night,* thinks the owl. *Tomorrow, I'll try again.*

Good Night, Earth

Life in the Shadows

Madagascar
Africa

Although darkness has fallen over Madagascar, the forest is still very much awake. Insects hum and chirp. Birds call to one another. Lemurs move through the trees.

But in one tree, there's a lemur that sits eerily still. His wide, orange saucer-shaped eyes gaze out, scanning the forest. Giant floppy ears stick up from his head. Amid his mostly dark fur, scattered strands of wiry white hair stick straight out. He is an aye-aye.

Life in the Shadows

The aye-aye begins to move, walking carefully along a branch. His long, knobbly fingers grip onto the bark. On his back, a bushy tail helps the lemur balance on the branch.

For some people who live on this island, the animal's spooky appearance brings fear. They see the primate as a sign of bad luck. One legend even says that if an aye-aye points its finger at someone, they will soon die. Because of this, the aye-aye could be killed just for being seen.

But the aye-aye is unaware of his supposed curse. Under the cover of darkness, he goes about his night.

Tap, tap, tap. With a long, slender middle finger, the aye-aye checks for grubs. They live in hollow spaces beneath the bark. "No luck," thinks the aye-aye. If the branch were hollow, it would make an echoing sound. The echo from the taps would let the aye-aye know to look deeper.

The aye-aye tries another branch. *Tap, tap.* Still no luck. He tries another, and another.

Finally, the aye-aye hears an echo. *There must be something inside,* he thinks. The aye-aye sinks his long middle finger into the bark and starts to dig. Then, he brings his mouth to the hole and rips away the loose bark with his teeth. He sticks his claw down into the hole, hooks a grub with his sharp nail, and swipes it up from the chiselled hole. Finally, he starts chewing. As he chews, the aye-aye plunges his finger back into the branch to dig some more.

Soon, the aye-aye hears a haunting cry that echoes across the forest. "Creeaye!" The aye-aye looks around. *That sound is familiar!* the he thinks. Then, he sees why. The cry came from another lemur. It was a warning! But for what?

Life in the Shadows

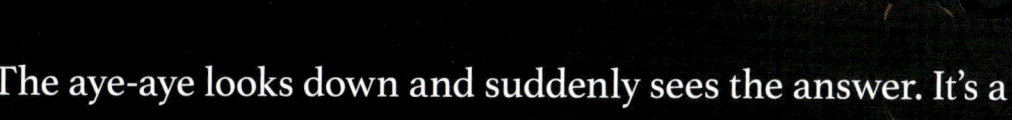

The aye-aye looks down and suddenly sees the answer. It's a human, and they are walking straight towards him.

He doesn't know that humans think aye-ayes are cursed. But he *does* know that being seen by a human could be dangerous. After all, humans are much bigger than aye-ayes!

The aye-aye freezes. Any movement could draw attention to him. But it doesn't matter. Soon, the aye-aye is blinded by a bright light. He turns to run away, but he can't see.

"It's OK," says a soothing voice. "I'm not here to hurt you."

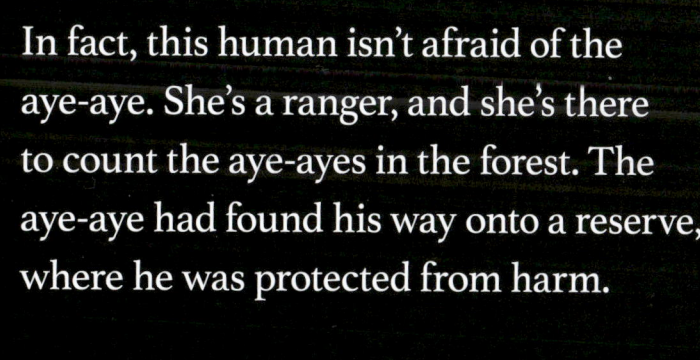

In fact, this human isn't afraid of the aye-aye. She's a ranger, and she's there to count the aye-ayes in the forest. The aye-aye had found his way onto a reserve, where he was protected from harm.

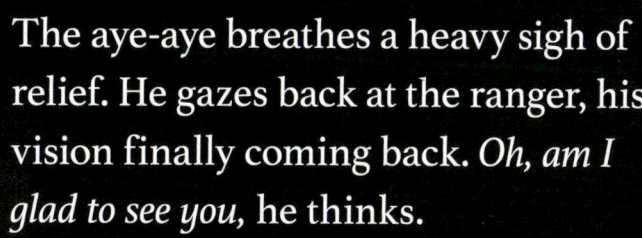

The aye-aye breathes a heavy sigh of relief. He gazes back at the ranger, his vision finally coming back. *Oh, am I glad to see you,* he thinks.

A Fancy Feast

NEW YORK CITY, UNITED STATES
NORTH AMERICA

The streets have grown quiet in New York City – or, at least, as quiet as they can be in the "city that never sleeps". Many people are in bed, resting for the day ahead. But yellow taxis still fill the roads, carrying passengers to and from their destinations. Locals and tourists still wander along the sidewalks, taking in the night air.

In Central Park, a lush green space in the middle of the city, calm has settled over the night. With no noisy streets or brightly lit buildings in sight, it's the perfect place for animals to rest. Some animals, including squirrels and birds, have just started their slumber, while others – such as raccoons – are just waking up.

A Fancy Feast

Amid the park's greenery, a family of four raccoons has been snoozing. They spent the day cuddled up inside a hollow log, unseen by people passing by. Joggers raced past on their daily runs. Tourists strolled by, maps in hand, looking for the nearby boathouse. Workers on their lunch breaks talked into their phones while quickly eating their food-cart fare.

Now, the raccoons climb out into the night. Using their noses to guide them, they make their way to the edge of the park. They run past a castle. They race under a stone archway. They cross over a bridge.

Finally, outside of the park, the raccoons cross the street, carefully dodging taxis. They scurry past streetlamps and neon-lit signs. Soon, they reach the aroma of a dark alley. *Score!* they think. *Time to eat!*

The raccoons set their eyes on a rubbish bin. With their agile hands, they quickly scale the side of it. One by one, they tumble inside. Carefully, they wade through the heap of rubbish.

It was a risky move to leave the park. But the raccoons are rewarded for their effort. The rubbish bin they've found is parked behind a fancy restaurant. Mounds of uneaten salads, steaks and vegetables sit on top of the rubbish pile. The raccoons dig into the food scraps with glee.

Good Night, Earth

Creak. Slowly, the back door of the restaurant opens, sending light pouring into the alley. *Let's get out of here!* one raccoon thinks. The rest of the raccoons have the same thought. As the door opens, the raccoons rush out of the rubbish bin and away from the alley.

A Fancy Feast

They run past the lampposts and neon signs, and across the street. Finally, they make their way back to the park and stop at a lake to take a quick drink before retreating into the bushes with their bellies full.

Good Night, Earth

A Wild Ride

INDIA
ASIA

The pangolin takes a cautious step up from its burrow. She pauses, listening for sounds from above. She hears nothing. *It's safe to come out,* thinks the pangolin. She takes a few more steps. At the top of the burrow entrance, she pauses again. This time, it's not to listen. Instead, she waits for her baby, who's still in the burrow. *Climb on!* her pause tells the baby.

The baby pangolin crawls onto his mum's tail and scoots his way up towards her back. With his thick, curved claws, the baby clings onto her tail's scaly sides.

A Wild Ride

Like a snake, the pangolin has scales. But these scales are much bigger and thicker. Each scale is made of a superstrong material called keratin. It's the same material in your fingernails! The scales are like armour for the animal. They protect the pangolins from predators.

With her baby locked on, the mum starts to walk through the forest. *Sniff, sniff.* Mum uses her strong sense of smell to search for insects. *Sniff, sniff, sniff.* She waves her head above the ground and detects ants in the ground. She stiffens her body as she gets ready to snack.

The young pangolin hops off his mum's tail. Then, she starts to dig, plunging her sharp front claws into the soil. Her back claws kick the dirt away.

The digging sends the ants running in all directions. But the mum stays calm. She slowly pokes out her long, sticky tongue. *Slurp!* She laps up dozens of ants. *Sluuuurp!* She grabs another dozen with her tongue.

While the pangolin snacks, a tiger has been lurking behind the forest brush. It's spotted the baby pangolin, and has been waiting for a chance to strike. *Now's the time to make my move,* thinks the tiger.

A WILD RIDE

Shwoop! The tiger lunges from the brush. It charges at the baby pangolin, mouth open and claws out. Frightened, the baby rolls himself into a little ball. His tail curls over his back. *My armor can protect me,* the baby thinks. But his scales are still growing, and they're no match for the tiger's sharp teeth.

Without hesitation, the mom jumps to action. She quickly grabs her baby with her claws and rolls him towards her. She pulls him to her belly and rolls into a bigger ball around him.

The tiger paws at the balled-up pangolins. Their bodies roll on the ground. But they stay curled up. Frustrated, the tiger crouches down and grabs the ball in between its big furry paws. It opens its mouth and tries to take a bite. But the armour is too thick to get through.

A Wild Ride

After a few minutes, the tiger retreats back into the forest. Finally, the pangolins unfurl. *That was scary,* thinks the baby pangolin. *I'm glad my mum was there to protect me!*

Shaken, the young pangolin crawls back onto his mum's tail. *That's enough ant hunting for one day,* the mum thinks. She walks her baby back to their burrow and they snuggle in.

Lights On!

Nature makes its own night-lights that illuminate the ground, water and sky. In some cases, the incredible bright lights are a survival tool. In others, the reason for their glow is still a mystery.

Good Night, Earth

Firefly Flashes

**Japan
Asia**

Lush green rice paddies line the countryside of Japan. For hundreds of years, farmers here have been growing rice in these fields. They plant rice seedlings in the soil. Then, they flood the beds with fresh water. These rice paddies hold the water so the seeds can grow. They're also where fireflies grow.

Firefly Flashes

Less than a year ago, a female firefly laid her eggs in the water of one of these rice paddies. Each egg glowed a dim green light. But one egg shone a little bit brighter than the others. Along with his siblings, the egg turned into a gleaming yellow-green larva. He started to crawl along the bottom of the paddy.

As the larva's body grew bigger, he shed his skin several times. When winter came, the water got too cold. Looking for warmth, the clever larva burrowed into the nearby soil. In the ground, he grew into a pupa. Then, he formed wings, came up from underground, and started to fly. He was now an adult.

In Japan, fireflies are called *hotaru*. Some believe that the *hotaru* are the souls of warriors who have died in battle. Because the fireflies use their light to find a mate, others see the insects as a symbol of love. Summertime festivals across the country celebrate the insects' arrival.

At night, couples gather to see the fireflies. They walk quietly along the boardwalks that border the rice paddies, holding hands as the sun sets.

As daylight dwindles above the rice paddies, the adult firefly joins dozens of others in the air. The sky gets darker, and soon thousands of fireflies are hovering above the paddies. Each one is looking for their perfect mate.

Frogs croak in the distance, while the fireflies are quiet. But their lights are like a symphony of messages to one another.

Now surrounded by a sea of lights, the firefly tries to look for a mate. He sends out a quick series of flickers. *Where are you?* he asks. He watches the ground and waits for a reply. No answer. He flies a bit further and tries asking again. Still no answer. The firefly is getting tired. It takes a quick rest in a nearby tree.

Slowly, as other fireflies find their mates, fewer and fewer lights can be seen in the air. But the firefly doesn't give up. He flies even further, and sends out another series of flickers.

Finally, a female who's been resting on a blade of grass sees the firefly's bright light standing out from the others. She returns a series of flashing lights. *Here I am!* she declares.

He sees her flashes and flies down to meet her on the ground. Now by her side, he lets out a twinkling flash. *Let's be friends,* he says.

As adults, fireflies only live for a few days. Although their time together is short, the time they share is celebrated by people far and wide.

Good Night, Earth

The Bay That Glows

Mosquito Bay, Puerto Rico
North America

"We're here!" yells the bus driver. A group of people step out of the bus and onto the sandy ground. The only light comes from the bus's headlights and the moon above. Each person on the beach walks to the water's edge and grabs a kayak. One by one, they climb in and push off into the dark water. Then the magic begins.

The Bay That Glows

The bus has dropped off visitors at the world's brightest bioluminescent bay. It's a shimmering secret along the coast of Vieques, a small Puerto Rican island. Below the water's surface, tiny organisms emit light.

It's called Mosquito Bay – but the area doesn't get its name from insects. Many years ago, this bay was a hiding place for a pirate ship named *El Mosquito*. No one knew why the waters glowed, but the pirates' enemies thought the bay held evil powers. They didn't dare to come near the ship.

The pirate ship is long gone, but the bay's eerie glow remains. Today, people from near and far travel to the bay to board kayaks and see the glow up close.

The bottoms of the kayaks are made of clear glass. When the boats enter the bay, the kayakers can see what's under their feet.

Near the shore, the water stays dark. It's too shallow for the organisms. But as the kayaks travel further into the bay, the movement of the paddles sparks the tiny organisms to life.

With each stroke of the paddles, the organisms send out brilliant flashes of light. As the kayaks pick up speed, it's as if millions of shooting stars are whizzing by.

Below the water's surface, the tiny organisms are not alone. Fish of many sizes also swim in the bay, including sharks and rays.

Stroke by stroke, the bay continues to shine. The light invites many fish to dine.

The Bay That Glows

A small fish swims up alongside one of the kayaks. The glow of the little organisms illuminates the fish's scales. Seeing the fish, the kayaker makes a sharp turn in the water to get out of the way. But the fish is hungry. It darts back towards the kayak, where the tiny organisms are still lighting up.

The small fish gets closer and closer, ready to snack on the little organisms. But then, an even bigger fish rushes up. The big fish is attracted by the glow. It scares away the smaller fish. The tiny organisms shine on.

Ghost Mushrooms

IRELAND
EUROPE

"Think we'll see any other ghosts on the trail?" one hiker jokes to another. "It *is* Halloween, after all!"

The hikers trod down a forest path, taking careful steps to avoid sinking into the muddy patches. One hiker carries a flashlight, illuminating the soggy trail ahead. They hadn't planned on hiking in the rain, but nature had other plans. Thankfully, the sheets over their bodies are keeping their clothes from getting *totally* soaked.

Suddenly, the flashlight goes out. "Uh-oh. Um . . . got any extra batteries in your pack?" the hiker asks. The other hiker shakes his head. "Well, we don't have a map either. I think we're . . . lost. And this rain isn't letting up. We should take cover until it stops."

"How about over there?" the other hiker points. "Under that tree. Race you there!"

The two hikers jog to a lush leafy tree just off the path. They duck underneath its branches. Carefully, they peel off their soggy sheets and take a deep breath. They look around, hoping to see a map or a sign to help them find their way out of the forest. Then, they see a faint glow that catches their eyes.

The glow is coming from the base of a nearby tree. "What is *that*?" the first hiker asks, squinting her eyes to see.

"It sure looks spooky! Should we take a closer look?" the second hiker eagerly asks.

Together they creep towards the light, treading slowly and carefully through the wet, leafy forest floor. With each step, they move deeper into the forest.

In European folklore, this kind of hovering light is a will-o'-the-wisp: a mysterious light made by mischievous spirits like fairies or ghosts. The supernatural lights supposedly have the power to lead wanderers astray, luring them into the forest with their eerie glow.

Ghost Mushrooms

Now standing in front of the light, the two hikers see what looks like a tiny pumpkin patch. Dozens of fist-sized orange disks stretch up from a decaying tree trunk. A neon-green glow comes from the underside of the disks and lights up the ground.

"I've read about these before! They're jack-o'-lantern mushrooms," the girl says.

"Oh, good! I was starting to get hungry," replies the boy. "I'll just grab a few . . ."

"Stop! No!" she yells. "They're poisonous!"

The curious hiker drops the mushroom. "Phew, that was close."

"Yeah, *too* close," the other hiker says, sighing with relief. Just then, the rain stops. In the distance, a sign comes into view. Now, the pair can finally find their way home.

And why were these mushrooms glowing? The answer is still a mystery to scientists. But the mushrooms help the forest by breaking down dead trees, making space for new plants to grow.

Mighty Mounds

Emas National Park, Brazil
South America

It's a hot, humid night in Emas National Park. Days ago, heavy rains soaked the flat, grassy savannah. Now, a maned wolf prowls through the tall grasses, waiting for a midnight snack. Nearby, a tall lump twinkles with tiny green lights. The formation looks like a festive Christmas tree. But there are no trees here. Above, a white-winged nightjar flies. The little bird comes to land on top of the lump.

Mighty Mounds

A closer look reveals that the lump is not a tree at all. It's a termite mound. There are many mounds across the savannah. Some of them are taller than people! And the lights are not decorations on a string. They are coming from tiny insects!

Termites built this mound. They gathered soil from the surrounding area. Little by little, they piled it up. They added their saliva and dung to the soil to make it stick together. Inside the mound, the walls have lots of tunnels. Air flows through these passages, so the inside of the mound is cool. The termites live under the mound.

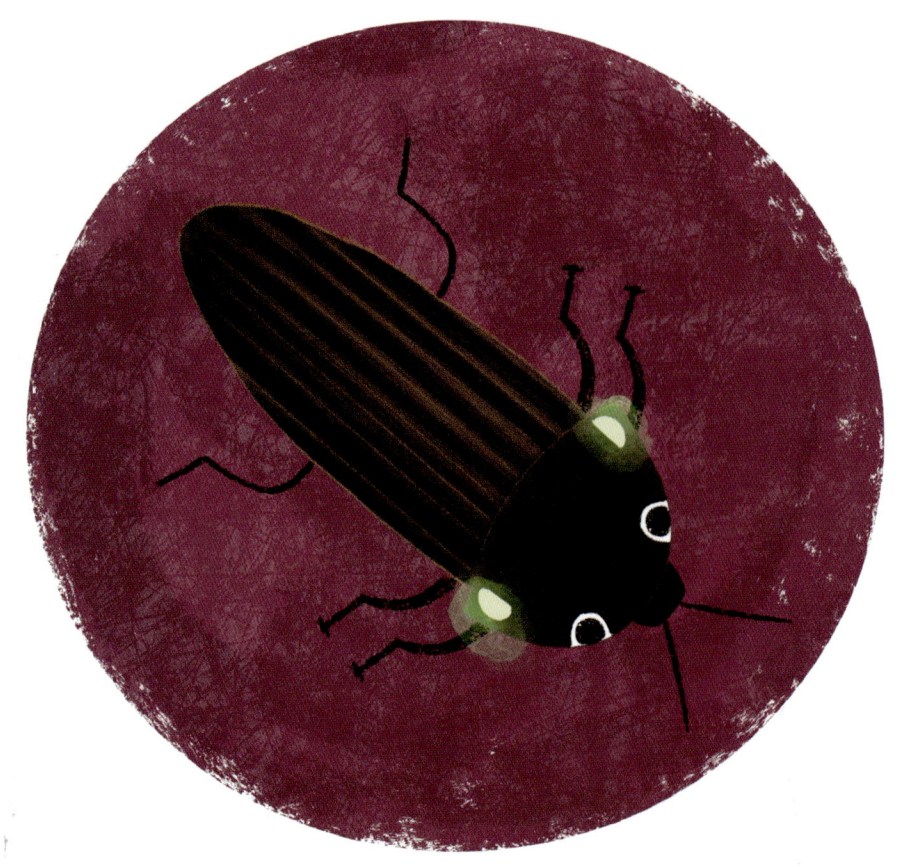

Although termites built this mound, another kind of insect lives here, too. It's the headlight beetle. Named for the two glowing dots on its back, this beetle lays dozens of eggs at once. The beetle places her eggs in the sides of the mound.

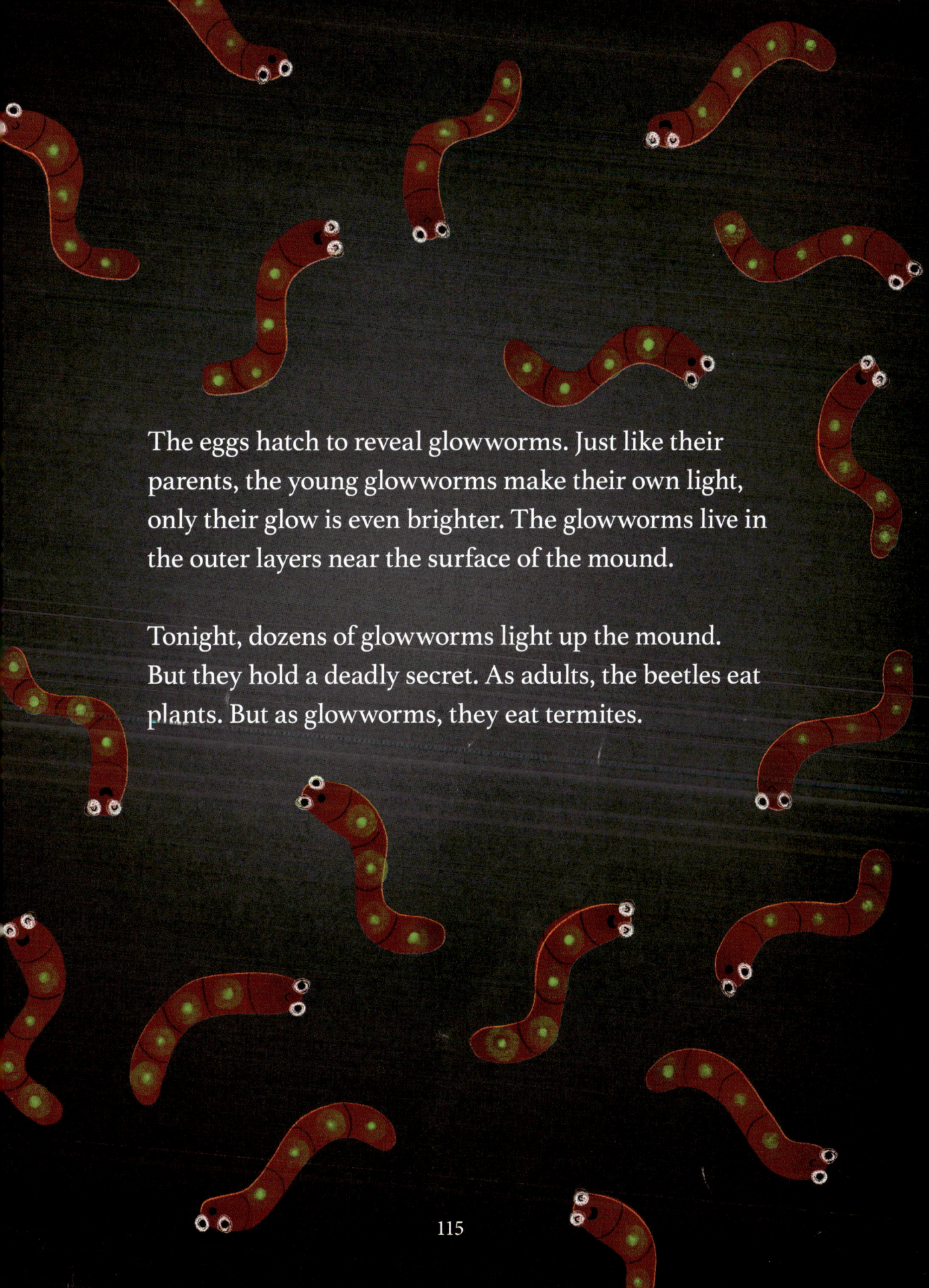

The eggs hatch to reveal glowworms. Just like their parents, the young glowworms make their own light, only their glow is even brighter. The glowworms live in the outer layers near the surface of the mound.

Tonight, dozens of glowworms light up the mound. But they hold a deadly secret. As adults, the beetles eat plants. But as glowworms, they eat termites.

Good Night, Earth

The glowworms' green light stays on all night. Patiently, they wait for termites to pass by. Soon, a heavy rain starts to fall from the sky. All across the savannah, the rain causes termites to take to the skies. They fly in all directions.

Some termites fly towards the mound. They're drawn to the eerie lights. They land on the side of the mound. *What's making this light?* they wonder. Curious, a termite crawls towards one of the mysterious lights.

Mighty Mounds

As the termite gets nearer, the glowworm creeps out of its hole and wiggles its body. The green light shimmers, encouraging the termite to come closer. The termite continues to walk towards the light. *Gotcha!* thinks the glowworm.

Whoosh! Quickly, the glowworm shoots out from the hole and grabs the termite with its jaws. It pulls the termite back into the hole. Then the glowworm devours it.

The other termites see the glowworm's trick unfold. *I'm not going to be next!* they think. The termites scatter back into the sky. The glowworms sent the termites an important message: looks can be deceiving.

Time to Grow

As nighttime unfolds, many plants bloom to life. Under the light of the moon, these plants have found clever and dazzling ways to survive and help their ecosystems thrive.

The Rimu's Rare Berries

New Zealand
Oceania

In a New Zealand forest, the rimu tree stretches up into the canopy. It has been standing for hundreds of years and is one of the tallest trees in the forest.

Its leaves, dangling from its branches, look like dripping strips of seaweed. At the tips of the leaves, green berries have just started to form. Soon, they will ripen and turn red. From the ground, the plentiful berries loom overhead.

The Rimu's Rare Berries

It's been a long time since the tree was this full of fruit. The rimu tree only grows this many berries every few years. When it does, it's good news for a bird called the kākāpō (cah-cah-POH).

The kākāpō is active at night and sleeps during the day. Tucked away on the forest floor, the bird can't get the vitamins it needs from sunlight. But the berries of the rimu tree are rich in the vitamins that help kākāpō chicks grow. When there aren't enough berries, the kākāpō won't have chicks.

For months, one kākāpō wondered, *Will I have chicks this year?* She looked to the rimu tree each night for an answer. She watched and waited to see if berries would fill the tree. Then, seeing the budding fruits, the answer was finally clear. *Yes, I will!* the kākāpō thought.

Night has fallen, and the kākāpō opens her eyes. She's been sleeping at the foot of the tree, nestled among its upturned roots. *Tonight is the night!* she thinks. *I'm going to check on those berries.* The large parrot moves slowly through the forest, headed straight for the rimu tree. She can't see very well, but the whisker-like feathers on her face help her feel around in the dark.

The kākāpō arrives at the tree. But she can't fly. She's too heavy and her wings are too short. To get to the berries, she has to climb the tree. She awkwardly scales the trunk, using her bill like an extra foot to grab hold. It takes some time, but she reaches the berries.

Up in the tree, the kākāpō leans forwards and grabs a bundle of leaves with her bill. She bites off a berry and – *boing!* – the leaves spring back. The kākāpō extends one of her legs and, with her sharp talons, grabs onto the leaves again. She's been waiting a long time for this meal. She quickly eats all of the berries in reach.

The Rimu's Rare Berries

Each night for the next few weeks, the kākāpō scales the tree and fills up on all the berries she can eat. But she knows that if she's going to have chicks, she'll need to find a mate.

One night, the kākāpō hears a deep, booming sound from a nearby hill. *Boom! Boom! Boom! Boom!* Then, she hears a high-pitched noise. *Ching! Ching! Ching!* She is drawn to the sounds. She walks up to find another kākāpō. He's dug a bowl-shaped hole in the ground so his calls will echo into the night. As she gets closer, she can smell a sweet scent on his feathers. She's found her mate. A few days later, she lays her eggs.

Back at the base of the tree where she sleeps, the kākāpō sits on three little eggs. She's dug a shallow hole in the soil to surround the eggs. Thanks to the vitamins she got from the rimu berries, the eggshells are thick and strong. For the next month, she will cover them and keep them warm.

The Rimu's Rare Berries

Protecting her eggs is an important job. Fewer than two hundred kākāpōs still live in these forests. When the eggs hatch, she will feed her fluffy white chicks the ripe berries from the rimu tree.

Blooms for Bats

ECUADOR
SOUTH AMERICA

Rocks curve and wind through the crevice carved into an Ecuadorian mountainside. The air is cold and wet inside the dark, quiet belly of the cave. Deep inside, icicle-shaped minerals called stalactites dangle from the cave ceiling. *Plunk.* A bead of water drips from a stalactite to the watery cave floor below. An eerie echo fills the air. *Plunk, plunk, plunk…*

Dark-brown specks dot the ceiling. From far away, these dots look like little rocks. But close-up, their furry bodies tell another story. Bats! The spooky site provides a resting space for the sleepy creatures.

Night is falling, and the sun rays that once filled the cave are slowly sinking away. The colony of Geoffroy's tailless bats begins to twitch to life. One by one, the upside-down bats slowly peel their eyes open. They stretch their wings to prepare for their nightly flight.

The bats begin to unlock their claws from the cave's ceiling. Suddenly, it's a race to the night sky. The frenzied bats rapidly flap their wings in an excited hurry to exit the cave and find a snack. Soon, the whole colony is bursting out of the cave's mouth.

Outside the cave, the bats swarm in the night sky. The further they get, the higher they fly.

As the journey grows longer, the bats fan out across the landscape. They follow the bends of the river, hoping to find some tasty treats.

Good Night, Earth

As the bats were waking up, a cactus was blooming to life. Miles away in the river valley, the large spiky cactus juts out from a grassy slope. Its many arms reach up towards the night sky. A dense clump of strange woolly hairs covers the side of one arm.

Amid the hairs, a small dark-pink bud opens to reveal a pale-yellow flower. Hundreds of bits of pollen stick straight out from the flower's centre, where a sweet nectar waits inside. The hairs surround the flower, protecting it from the hot sun during the day. But at night, these hairs have another special job. They help the hungry bats find the flower's nectar. The bats can't see the flower well in the dark, so they must rely on other senses to find their snack.

Soon, one of the bats approaches the cactus. *Chirp, chirp, chirp!* The bat sends out a high-pitched noise. The curious creature's leaf-shaped nose directs the sound waves outwards. The sound waves reach the cactus. Like dry soil absorbs water, the hairs absorb the sound waves. But the flower in the middle bounces the sound back.

The bat's big ears detect the flower's echo. *I must be close!* thinks the bat. It drops lower towards the bloom. As the bat gets closer, the flower's sweet scent confirms the bat is in the right place. *Finally, I've found a snack!*

Excited, the bat zooms towards the flower. Look out! The bat loses control of its speed and crashes into the cactus. Its wings slam into prickly spines. *Ouch!* thinks the bat. It quickly jerks backwards in midair, away from the painful plant. Furiously beating its wings, the bat hovers timidly above the tiny flower.

Carefully now, it flies in a little closer, then closer. The bat sticks out its tongue, preparing to finally take a drink. Face-first into the flower it flies, slurping up the bloom's sweet nectar. Pollen sticks to the bat's snout as it plunges deeper and deeper into the tasty flower.

Finished with its snack, the bat flies away, its long nose still powdered with pollen. Without knowing it, the bat is doing an important job. It sprinkles the pollen across the river valley as it flies. If the pollen falls in the right place, someday it could turn into new plants. That would mean more flowers for future bats.

There are still many hours left in the night. The bat soars back into the sky, rejoining the other bats in the colony. A symphony of chirps fills the air. There are more cactus plants to be found, and more flowers to snack on before sunrise.

Good Night, Earth

A Sparkling Surprise

Mediterranean Coast, Greece
Europe

Tonight, a full moon hangs in the sky above a Greek island, casting its glow over a rocky field. The clear blue water of the Mediterranean Sea splashes up against the cliff with each crashing wave.

At the top of the cliff, overlooking the sea, a plant has been quietly growing. The tall, sprawling shrub is covered in hundreds of round pinkish-red cones. Most nights, insects fly past. But not on this night.

A Sparkling Surprise

The shrub has been patiently waiting for this full moon. Tonight, with the weather warm and the moon bright, is the best night of the year for insects to visit. *I've got to get their attention,* the plant thinks. *Now is my chance to shine!*

Slowly, the shrub's reddish cones ooze beads of clear liquid. Under the full moon, the liquid catches the light. The cones begin to sparkle like diamonds.

Inside, each shimmering bead holds a sweet surprise. The liquid is a sugary nectar. It's a tasty treat for any insects that stop by. Bits of pollen from the visiting insect make their way into the nectar.

A Sparkling Surprise

Down the road, the nearby town is quiet and still. The tavernas have closed, the boats have docked, and the people are asleep. A line of streetlamps illuminates the empty road. The only movement in sight comes from a moth fluttering below one of the lamps.

The moth was on his nightly flight when he got sidetracked. For nearly an hour, he has been frantically flying in circles around the lamp. The moth is confused. He thinks that the light is coming from the moon.

Like many insects, the moth will use the moonlight as a guide. He will position his back to the light, so he knows which way to fly. But this light doesn't move with him. When he gets a few feet away, the light grows dimmer.

I must be going the wrong way, the moth thinks. He twists and turns in the air. *Which way is up?* the moth wonders as he starts to panic.

Zeeeep! Just then, the bulb inside the lamp burns out. Finally, the moth can clearly see the moonlight. He flies away from the unlit lamp. He aims his back to the moon and starts to fly towards the rocky field.

A Sparkling Surprise

Now that the moth has found the moonlight, he soars past houses and roads. He flies over the field. Soon, he comes to the rocky cliff. He sees the shimmering droplets down below.

The moth flies down to get a closer look. He lands on a sticky cone, and his feet sink into a sparkling bead. He drinks up the sweet nectar.

That was delicious! the moth thinks. The nectar gives the moth energy to continue his nighttime flight. He flies away, his legs still wet with nectar.

Short and Sweet

TEXAS, UNITED STATES
NORTH AMERICA

"It's 8 o'clock," says the boy. "Time to go out to the garden!"

"OK, OK," the girl grumbles. "But I'm not holding my breath." She grabs her camera. "Let's go."

Recently, the twins' grandmother had planted some flowers in the garden – common evening primroses, to be exact. But there were no flowers yet, only buds. She told them that the buds would only bloom after the sun went down, and that they had to be patient. For weeks the siblings had been coming to the garden every night, hoping to finally see one of the flowers bloom.

"I don't know why you think tonight will be any different than the last 20," the girl says, rolling her eyes.

"The flowers have to show up soon!" the boy protests. "Grandma said if we watch for long enough, we'll see something really special."

So the twins sit on the stairs leading down to the backyard, and they wait. And they wait some more. The summer air in their Texas neighbourhood is thick and warm.

Some 45 minutes go by, and the sun starts to set over the yard. Then, they see a twitch. They stand up and walk to the plant.

"The bud!" the girl whispers with excitement. "It's shaking!" The boy leans in to get a better look. Sure enough, a bud is starting to quiver under the setting sun.

The twins eagerly watch. Slowly, the petals begin to unfurl. After a few minutes, four yellow heart-shaped petals appear. Then, a subtle scent of lemon fills the air, signalling its arrival to nearby insects. It wafts from the bright-yellow bowl-shaped bloom up to the twins' noses.

Short and Sweet

"Wow, it finally happened!" the boy says. "And it smells just like Grandma said it would!"

"I have to admit, that is pretty cool," the girl says, trying to hide her enthusiasm.

Flash! The girl snaps a photo of the flower in bloom. "There," she says. "Now we can show Grandma what we saw."

Satisfied with their first flower sighting, the twins go to sleep.

GOOD NIGHT, EARTH

The next night, Grandma comes to visit the twins. Earlier, they had sent her the photo and asked her to come see for herself. They walk her back into the garden, eager to show her the new bloom. But the petals, once wide and bright, are now withered and closed.

"But . . . I don't understand!" the girl cries with disappointment. "It was *just* here! You saw the picture!"

"I know," Grandma says. She looks lovingly at the twins. There was something she still hadn't told them about these special flowers. Now was the time.

"You see, kids," Grandma says. "These flowers don't stay open for very long. Usually, they bloom for only a day or two."

"But that's not long at all!" the boy protests. "And we waited so long to see one!"

"I know," Grandma says again. "It's not fair, is it? But that doesn't mean we can't enjoy them for the short time that we have them."

"I guess you're right," the girl says. "So . . . what do we do now?"

"Well, why don't we see what tonight will bring?" Grandma suggests. So together, the three of them sit down on the steps and wait for more flowers to bloom.

A Midnight Sky

The night sky is full of surprises! On clear nights, the moon and stars seem to guide animals across darkened landscapes. Sometimes, auroras and moonbows paint beautiful colours overhead, or meteors sparkle like diamonds as they shoot across the sky.

Good Night, Earth

Into the Sea

Great Barrier Reef, Australia
Oceania

The stars in the Australian sky seem to twinkle and dance. Above the beach, far from city lights, they shine brightly in the darkness. Amid the glimmering lights, a crescent moon hangs low.

Below the sky, where the dunes line the edge of the beach, a clutch of sea turtles is nestled in a hole in the sand.

Into the Sea

For weeks, the turtles have been tucked away, hidden from view, protecting their babies as they grow inside eggshells.

Tonight, the temperature outside is finally right. Like the bubbles in a pot of boiling water, the eggs tremble and shake. *Boop! Boop! Boop!* With the pokes of their heads, the babies break open their shells. They stretch their front flippers through the shells and pull their tiny bodies out into the nest.

Good Night, Earth

During the day, dozens of people dot the sandy beach between the dunes and the sea. They eat picnics and play games and make castles in the sand. But after the sun sets, the beach grows empty. A soft breeze cools the quiet night air as the ocean waves roll onto the shore.

Now, the babies are big and strong enough to crawl. Just as they pulled themselves out of their shells, now they pull themselves out of their nest. The baby turtles crawl over each other in a race to the sea. One by one, they reach the top of the nest as the moonlight hits their faces.

Into the Sea

Crawl towards me, little turtles, the moon seems to say.

So the babies crawl. *Flip-fop. Flip-flop.* With each movement of their flippers, the babies quickly race to the water.

The light from the moon and stars reflects onto the water. The hatchlings form a group for protection against predators as they crawl down the sandy slope towards the light-soaked sea.

The hatchlings scurry as fast as they can. They are small, and they know that the journey is a risk. Birds or other animals could easily eat them. They must move quickly.

But the closer the babies get, the more tired they become. One of them, in her frenzied pace, races over a small mound and somersaults into the sand. Lying on her back, she almost gives up. But she musters the strength to flip her belly back onto the sand. And she sees the moon once again.

Just a few more steps! the moon seems to say to her now. With the finish line in sight, she makes the last few steps towards the sea.

A wave gently rolls over the baby as she enters the water. For a moment, the water pushes the turtle back towards the beach. She pushes and fights against the wave, trying to propel herself forwards.

As the wave ebbs back into the ocean, it carries the baby with it. She's finally made it to the sea!

Years from now, once again at nighttime, the turtles will return to this beach. They will swim back onto the shore, crawl back to the dunes, and make their own nests to lay eggs in.

Good Night, Earth

Roll With It

Southern Africa

The moon above the African grassland glows bright. Just below, a band of light made of billions of stars stretches across the sky. It's called the Milky Way.

Earlier today, a herd of elephants was grazing on the grassy plain. They feasted on the lush buffet of greens. When they were finished, they left behind giant, stinky heaps of dung!

Now, under the starry sky, dozens of beetles have sniffed out the fresh dung. This is what they eat! A few of them land on the same giant clump. Each beetle gets to work on collecting some of the dung.

The first beetle to arrive tugs at the clump of dung with his front legs. He pulls at the clump and breaks off a smaller piece. As other beetles start to arrive, he pushes the dung through the dirt to get it nice and round. Finally, he forms the perfect ball.

Roll a ball? Check. Time to make my getaway! the male beetle thinks. He crawls down the ball so his front legs touch the ground. He keeps his other legs on the ball and starts to push backwards.

A female beetle sees the rolled-up dung. "Wow, that's a great ball!" she thinks. She crawls on top of it. Neither one of the beetles knows where they are headed. But they will go there together.

The strong beetle starts to roll his ball away from the dung pile, guided by the moon and stars. On nights like this, when the sky is clear and bright, the beetles can sense the moon's light and starlight from above. The light leads the beetles in a straight line out of the pile.

Suddenly, a patch of thick clouds floats overhead. It dims the light from the moon and stars. The sudden change sends the dung beetle spinning. Without the lights to guide him, he is lost. *Bump! Bump!* He starts to roll in circles, moving this way and that way as the ball crashes into other dung balls on the move.

Amid the confusion, another beetle rushes towards the dung ball. He wants to steal it! The roller beetle pushes the charging beetle back. The charging beetle tries again, and again the roller pushes back. After a few rounds, the sneaky beetle gives up.

Good Night, Earth

Soon, the clouds pass. With the glow of the moon and stars back in view, the beetle is back on track. He pushes the dung ball far beyond the dung heap. He keeps going until there are no other beetles in sight.

This looks like a good spot, the female beetle thinks. She hops off the dung ball and starts to dig into the soft ground. The male starts to dig with her. Once the hole is deep enough, they roll the ball into the hole.

As the beetles dig, they detect a flash, then another. A meteor shower has begun! It sprinkles shooting stars across the sky, as if the sky is celebrating the beetle's victory.

Finally, the female beetle lays an egg inside the ball of dung. The parents will take turns watching their dung ball. They will keep watch until the egg hatches. When it does, the baby beetles will feast on the dung.

Painted Skies

ENONTEKIÖ, FINLAND
EUROPE

In northern Finland, the sun has set and temperatures have dropped. Snow-covered mountains loom above the tundra. Harsh, frigid winds blow across the icy ground. The closest town is many miles away. With no lights from city streets, the tundra is cloaked in darkness. The stars and the moon provide the only source of light across the arctic landscape.

At the base of the mountain range, a fox has emerged from a nearby pine forest. This is no ordinary fox. It's a magical fire fox! According to a Finnish myth, the fire fox has the power to create colourful streaks of light that shimmer across the sky. These streaks are known as the Northern Lights, or aurora borealis. On clear nights between September and April, skygazers in the Northern Hemisphere can catch a glimpse of this light show in action. From May to August on the other side of the world, the aurora australis, or Southern Lights, is equally dazzling.

The fox's fiery red hair stands out against the snowy white landscape. As the hungry fox perches on a rock, it scans its surroundings. At first, the tundra is still and silent. It's as if the land is frozen in time. Suddenly, the fox hears a distant rustling noise. *Shh!* The fox freezes in its tracks. Where did the sound come from? The fox tilts its head, angling one ear down to listen.

There! Beyond the mountains, beneath the snow! thinks the fox. *It must be a lemming!* The small rodent is a favourite snack for foxes in this arctic place. The fox continues to listen, waiting for the perfect moment to strike. But how will it get across the mountains? The magical creature knows a secret way.

Whoosh! The fire fox leaps into the sky. Now as big as the clouds, the giant animal races towards the sound, springing from one mountain peak to the next. With each jump, the fox's bushy tail bobs up and down. Quickly, the fox ascends higher and higher.

As the fox leaps onto the tallest peak, its tail dips down, brushing against the powdery snow. When the fiery red tail meets the frozen ground, the contact creates a brilliant green spark. Like a magnificent explosion of fireworks, the spark bursts into the night sky.

In an instant, the single spark ignites a glowing streak of neon-green that shoots across the sky. More green ribbons of light glow to life around it, bending and swirling in perfect harmony. The scene looks like an otherworldly watercolour painting coming to life.

Soon, a swirling rainbow illuminates the dark starry canvas. The curtains of colour – first green, then red, then pink and violet – dance across the sky like waves rolling across the ocean towards the shore.

Good Night, Earth

It's as if the dancing lights are celebrating the fox's quest. But the animal is too busy to notice the beautiful scene just yet. It is still on the hunt. Using its powerful hind legs, the fox leaps upwards from the tip of the mountaintop. Twisting its body in midair, the cunning creature pivots downwards. As the fox descends from the sky, its body shrinks back to its normal size.

Crunch! The fox's face plummets snout-first into the densely packed snow. For a moment, the creature's head is buried in the icy ground. Then . . . success! The fox yanks its head up from the snow, grasping the lemming tightly in its teeth. *Time to eat!*

PAINTED SKIES

With the chase over and its belly full, the fox finally gazes up at the sky. Now that the hunt is over, the fox can enjoy the show. For a few moments, the animal watches with pride as the aurora continues to dance. Then, it begins the long walk back to the forest. With each step of the fox's fur-padded paws, the night sky grows darker and darker. Finally, the magical creature retreats into the forest. Among the snow-covered trees, the fox sits down to rest beside a fallen tree.

As the fox stills, the colourful streamers of light fully fade from the sky. Now, once again, only the moon and stars illuminate the night. The fox curls its fluffy tail around its body for warmth, satisfied with the day's work, and settles in to sleep.

A Magical Mist

Victoria Falls, Zimbabwe
Africa

Boom! Crash! The summer thunderstorms were unrelenting. For months, they poured rain over southern Africa, soaking the forests and helping plants grow. Much of the rain filtered through the soggy ground and made its way to the Zambezi River. As each day passed, the water in the river grew higher and higher.

A Magical Mist

Now confined by the riverbanks, the water has nowhere to go but through. So it pushes forwards, its strong current rapidly gushing towards the Indian Ocean.

Along the path, the rushing water meets Victoria Falls – one of the world's largest waterfalls. Here, at the top, it faces a giant hurdle – a sudden, unexpected drop.

Tonight, a full moon hangs low in the sky. It casts a brilliant steady light across the rushing water. It quietly gazes over the scene.

A Magical Mist

As the water rushes towards the looming cliff, it faces the unknown. But the moon's glow illuminates what is to come. Over the edge of the fall, the water will make a long and perilous plunge. Not all of it will make it.

The water gushes off the cliff and into the gorge far below. *Whooooosh!* It slams towards the ground. As it falls, the water transforms into a huge curtain in front of the cliff. It picks up speed as it plunges, trapping air and turning a frothy white.

But some of the droplets break away from the falling curtain and bounce up towards the moon. As the droplets meet the warm air they turn to mist.

A Magical Mist

The moon's light shines onto the misty droplets floating above the fall. When the moonlight and droplets meet, a magnificent moonbow arcs across the waterfall, forming a floating bridge from the top of the cliff to base.

The rest of the water charges onwards, gathering speed as it rushes to the base. The drop seems never-ending. But waiting at the base of the fall is a pool of water. Here, under the moon's steady glow, the water that reaches the bottom finally rests.

Say "Good Night" Around the World

How do people say "good night" in other languages? Find out below.
Can you try saying some of these phrases?

Buona notte
(bwo-nah noh-teh)
Italian

Selamat tidur
(suh-lah-mat tee-dur)
Indonesian

Сайн шөнө
Sain shöno
(sign shoh-noh)
Mongolian

Buenas noches
(bweh-nahs noh-chehs)
Spanish

शुभ रात्रि
Shubh raatri
(shoo-bh rah-tree)
Hindi

Tafandria mandry
(tah-fan-dree-uh man-dree)
Malagasy

İyi geceler
(ee-yee geje-lehr)
Turkish

Tusbih ealaa khayr
(too-sbee eye-lah high-er)
Arabic

Oyasuminasai
(oh-yah-soo-mee-nah-sigh-ee)
Japanese

Goeie nag
(khoo-yeh nakh)
Afrikaans

Boa noite
(bow-ah noy-chay)
Brazilian Portuguese

Hyvää yötä
(hee-vah-ah yoh-tah)
Finnish

**Καληνύχτα
Kalinýchta**
(kah-lee-nee-chtah)
Greek

Pō mārie
(poh mah-ree-eh)
Māori

Wǎn ān (uan ahn)
Mandarin Chinese

Magandang gabi
(mah-gan-dang gah-bee)
Tagalog

Chúc ngủ ngon
(chook ngoo ngawn)
Vietnamese

Bonne nuit
(bon nwee)
French

Gute Nacht
(goo-teh nakt)
German

Jal jayo
(jahl jeye-yo)
Korean

Usiku mwema
(oo-see-koo mweh-mah)
Swahili

Did You Know . . . ?

KOALAS can sleep up to 22 hours a day.

Sleeping **HIPPOS** can surface to the water to breathe without waking up.

The **AYE-AYE** is the world's largest nocturnal primate.

During hibernation, the average **BROWN BEAR** only breathes once every 45 seconds.

Young **RED-EYED TREE FROGS** can change their colour based on the time of day.

STARLINGS likely get their name from the pointy star shape of their bodies in flight.

NURSE SHARKS rest in groups of up to 40 along the seafloor.

GIRAFFES can sleep while standing up. They only need 30 minutes of sleep a day.

The black "mask" around a **RACCOON**'s eyes absorbs light to help the animal see more clearly.

NILE CROCODILES sleep with only half their brain resting. This means they can keep one eye open to watch for threats or prey.

ARCTIC FOXES wrap their tails around their bodies like blankets while they snooze.

DUNG BEETLES use the light of the Milky Way as a compass to navigate in the dark.

OWLS have special feathers that allow them to fly silently in the night sky.

ORANGUTANS build a new nest every night.

When sleeping, **SEA TURTLES** tuck themselves into reefs or under rocks to hide from predators.

WORKER ANTS take hundreds of minute-long naps throughout each day.

MOTHS confuse streetlights for the moon, which they follow during migration.

In Finland, some **AURORAS** have made whooshing and popping noises.

At night, you can see the bright lights of **NEW YORK CITY**'s Times Square from space.

Capsule hotels, where guests sleep in stacks of bed-sized pods, are common in some parts of **JAPAN**.

To help them see at night, **TARSIERS** – found in Borneo and other parts of Southeast Asia – have eyes that are as big as their brain.

Halloween originated in **IRELAND** as a festival known as Samhain, which marked the end of summer and the beginning of the "dark half" of the year.

In the warmer months, a colony of 1.5 million **FREE-TAILED BATS** emerge nightly from their roost under a bridge in Austin, Texas.

In winter, the most northern parts of **CANADA** spend weeks without daylight.

To plan their farming and hunting, the Māori in **NEW ZEALAND** formulated a calendar based on the phases of the moon.

Kicking off at night, parades in **BRAZIL** celebrating Carnival can last until sunrise.

Filled with millions of glowing microorganisms, **PUERTO RICO'S MOSQUITO BAY** is the world's brightest bioluminescent bay.

Glossary

AURORA A natural display of lights caused by particles colliding near Earth's poles

BIOLUMINESCENCE The ability of a living organism (such as a firefly) to produce its own light through chemical reactions

BURROW A hole or tunnel in the ground that is dug by an animal and used for shelter

CANOPY A dense layer of a rainforest made up of overlapping trees and branches, where many animals live

COLONY A group of animals, such as ants, that live and work together

CONE A scaly part of a plant that contains pollen or seeds

DEN A shelter or resting place for an animal

KERATIN A type of protein that helps to form animal hair, nails and skin

LARVA A stage of an animal's development in which its appearance differs from its adult form

MIGRATION The movement of animals from one place to another, usually during a certain time each year

MILKY WAY The cluster of stars, gas, dust and planets that make up our solar system

MOONBOW A colourful arc in the sky formed by light from the moon

NECTAR A sweet liquid produced by plants to attract insects and other animals

NOCTURNAL Active at night and asleep during the day

PADDY A field that has been flooded and is being used to grow certain crops, such as rice

POLLEN A powdery substance produced by some plants to help make new seeds

WILDFIRE An uncontrolled fire in a natural area, such as a forest or grassy field, that can spread quickly

Index

A
Alaska 48–53
aurora borealis 158–163
Australia 22–27, 146–151
aye-aye 74–79

B
bats 126–131
bears 48–53
beetles 114–117, 152–157
bioluminescent bay 100–105
Borneo 36–41
Botswana 10–15
Brazil 112–117

C
cactus flower 128–131
Canada 28–33
China 68–73
common evening primroses 138-143
Costa Rica 62–67

D
dung beetles 152–157

E
Ecuador 126–131
elephant dung 152–157

F
Falkland Islands 54–59
Finland 158–163
fire fox 158–163
fireflies 94–99
frogs 62–67

G
glowworms 115–117
Greece 132–137

H
headlight beetles 114–115
hippos 10–15

I
India 86–91
Ireland 106–111
Italy 16–21

J
Japan 94–99
jerboa 68–73

K
kākāpō 121–125
koala 22–27

L
lemurs 74–79

M
Madagascar 74–79
Magellanic penguins 54–59
meerkats 42–47
moth 135–137
mushrooms 106–111

N
New York City 80–85
New Zealand 120–125
Northern Lights 158–163

O
orangutans 36–41
otters 28–33
owl 70–73

P
pangolins 86–91
penguins 54–59
Puerto Rico 100–105

R
raccoons 80–85
rimu berries 120–125
Rome, Italy 16–21

S
sea turtles 146–151
South Africa 42–47
Southern Africa 152–157
starlings 16–21

T
termites 112–117
Texas 138–143
tiger 88–91
turtles 146–151

V
Victoria Falls, Zimbabwe 164-169

Z
Zimbabwe 164–169

Author: Rose Davidson
Project Editor: Priyanka Lamichhane
Illustrator: Ester Gouw
Designer: Alice Seiler
Publishing Director: Piers Pickard
Publisher: Rebecca Hunt
Art Director: Andy Mansfield
Print Production: Nigel Longuet

Published in September 2025
by Lonely Planet Global Limited
CRN: 554153
ISBN: 978-1-83758-479-6
www.lonelyplanet.com/kids
© Lonely Planet 2025
10 9 8 7 6 5 4 3 2 1
Printed in China

All rights reserved. No part of this publication may be reproduced, stored in a retrieval system, or transmitted in any form by any means, electronic, mechanical, photocopying, recording, or otherwise except brief extracts for the purpose of review, without the written permission of the publisher. Lonely Planet and the Lonely Planet logo are trademarks of Lonely Planet and are registered in the US Patent and Trademark Office and in other countries.

Although the author and Lonely Planet have taken all reasonable care in preparing this book, we make no warranty about the accuracy or completeness of its content and, to the maximum extent permitted, disclaim all liability from its use.

Stay in Touch
lonelyplanet.com/contact

Lonely Planet Office:
IRELAND
Digital Depot, Roe Lane (off Thomas St), Digital Hub, Dublin 8, D08 TCV4, Ireland